Presented to

_____

By

_____

On the Occasion of

_____

Date

_____

CHARLES COLSON

The Line Between

Right & Wrong

*Developing a Personal
Code of Ethics*

BARBOUR
PUBLISHING, INC.
Uhrichsville, OH

Published by   Barbour Publishing, Inc.
              P.O. Box 719
              Uhrichsville, Ohio 44683
              http://www.barbourbooks.com

Member of the
Evangelical Christian
Publishers Association

Printed in the United States of America.

THE PROBLEM OF ETHICS

Harvard well deserves its reputation as a very liberal university—liberal in the best sense of the word—because you have as a lecturer in the university today someone who is an ex-convict.

Harvard also deserves the reputation for being a liberal university, in the best sense of the word, because over the last three years, I have written articles that here at Harvard could be considered quite impertinent, in which I have described my views on why it is impossible to teach ethics at Harvard. And you've invited me to speak anyway.

I'm no longer in politics. I've done my time, literally and figuratively. But it's awfully hard not to watch what is happening on the political scene without a certain sense of dismay. Look at the Keating Five—five United States senators, tried, in effect, by their own

5

tribunal. Just before that, Senator Dave Durenberger, who happens to be a good friend of mine, was censured by the Senate. I also spent some time with Marion Barry, the former mayor of the District of Columbia, who was arrested for drug use. And in South Carolina and Arizona, scams in the legislatures have been exposed by federal prosecutors.

I saw a press release in which the Department of Justice boasted that last year they had prosecuted and convicted 1,150 public officials, the highest number in the history of the republic. They were boasting about it, yet I read it with a certain sadness because it seems that kind of corruption has become epidemic in American politics.

We have seen congressmen, one after another: Coehlo, Wright, Frank, Lukens—both sides of the aisle—either being censured or forced out of office. We see probably the most cynical scandal of all—the HUD scandal—

CHARLES COLSON
The Line Between
Right
&
Wrong

where people were ripping off money from the public treasury that was designed to help the poor. Then, we've seen more spy scandals during the past five years than in all previous 195 years of American history combined—people selling their national honor for sexual favors or for money.

Business is not immune. The savings and loan scandals are bad enough on the face of them, but the fact that they're so widespread has fostered almost a looter's mentality. Ivan Boesky, speaking at UCLA Business School five years ago, said, "Greed is a good thing," and ended up spending three years in a federal prison. Just last week one of the major pharmaceutical firms was fined $10 million for covering up violations of criminal statutes.

It affects athletics. If you picked up a newspaper this week, you saw that Sugar Ray Leonard has just admitted to drug use. He's been a role model for lots of kids on the street.

I BELIEVE

WE ARE EXPERIENCING

TODAY IN OUR COUNTRY

WHAT I CHOOSE TO CALL

A CRISIS

OF CHARACTER.

Pete Rose spent time in prison for gambling.

Academia has been affected. Stanford University's President Kennedy was charged with spending $7,000 to buy a pair of sheets—they must be awfully nice bed linens—and charging them improperly to a government contract. One day a Nobel Prize winner was exposed for presenting a fraudulent paper, and the very next day a professor at Georgetown University was charged with filing a fraudulent application for a grant from the National Institutes of Health. Probably saddest of all, at least from my perspective, are the cases of certain religious leaders like Jimmy Swaggart and Jim Bakker. Bakker—whom I've also visited in prison—was prosecuted for violating what should be the most sacred trust of all: to speak for God and to minister to people in their spiritual needs.

The first question that comes to mind is whether these are simply examples of rotten

CHARLES COLSON
The Line Between
Right & Wrong

9

apples or of better prosecutors. Maybe you can dismiss these by saying, "this is simply the nature of humanity." I think it was Bishop Fulton Sheen, in paraphrasing G.K. Chesterton, who once said that the doctrine of original sin is the only philosophy empirically validated by 3,500 years of human history. Maybe you dismiss this, too, and say, "this is just the way people are."

But is there a pattern here?

Time magazine, in its cover story on ethics, said what's wrong: "Hypocrisy, betrayal and greed unsettle a nation's soul." The *Washington Post* said that the problem has reached the point where "common decency can no longer be described as common." The *New Republic* magazine said, "There is a destructive sense that nothing is true and everything is permitted."

I submit to you that when the *Washington Post,* the *New Republic* magazine, and *Time* magazine—which have never been know as bastions of conservative, biblical morality—begin to talk about some sort of ethical malaise, a line has been crossed. These aren't simply isolated instances, but rather a pattern emerging in American life.

No institution has been more sensitive to this than Harvard. Former President Bok has given some extraordinary speeches decrying the loss of ethics in the American business community. I think some of you have seen the recent polls finding that business school students across America, by a two-to-one margin, believe that businesses are generally unethical. It's a very fragile consensus that holds together trust in our institutions. When most business school students believe there aren't any ethical operations, you begin to wonder if something isn't affecting us a lot more broadly than isolated instances of misbehavior that have been exposed.

I believe we are experiencing today in our

CHARLES COLSON
The Line Between
Right & Wrong

11

I BELIEVE WE SHOULD
BE DEEPLY CONCERNED
ABOUT THE LOSS OF. . .
THE TRADITIONAL VALUES OF
REPUBLICAN CITIZENSHIP—
WORDS LIKE VALOR, HONOR,
DUTY, RESPONSIBILITY,
COMPASSION, CIVILITY.

country what I choose to call a crisis of character: a loss of those inner restraints and virtues that prevent Western civilization from pandering to its own darker instincts.

If you look back through the history of Harvard, you'll see that President Elliott was as concerned about the development of character as he was about education. Plato once said, if you asked why we should educate someone, "we educate them so that they become a good person, because good persons behave nobly." I believe we should be deeply concerned about the loss of what Edmund Burke called the traditional values of republican citizenship —words like valor, honor, duty, responsibility, compassion, civility. Words which sound quaint when uttered in these surroundings.

Why has this happened? I'm sure many of you studied philosophy in your undergraduate courses, and, if so, you are well aware that, through twenty-three centuries of Western

CHARLES COLSON
The Line Between
Right Wrong

civilization, we were guided by a shared set of assumptions that there was a transcendent value system. This was not always the Judeo-Christian value system, though I think the Judeo-Christian values were, as the eminent historian Christopher Dawson wrote, "the heart and soul of Western civilization."

It goes back to the Greeks and Plato's saying that if there were no transcendent ideals, there could be no concord, justice, and harmony in a society. There is through twenty-three centuries of civilization—the history of the West—a strain of belief in a transcendent value system. Whether it was the unknown god of the Greeks, the Christ of the Scriptures revealed to the Christian, Yahweh of the Old Testament revealed to the Jew, or, as Enlightenment thinkers chose to call it, natural law—which I believe to be not inconsistent with Judeo-Christian revelation—this belief guided our conduct for twenty-three centuries until a great cultural revolution began in America.

CHARLES COLSON
The Line Between
Right & Wrong

This revolution took place in our country in the 1960s. Some think it goes back further. Paul Johnson—who happens to be one of my favorite historians—wrote a history of Christianity, a history of the Jew, and a classic book called *Modern Times*. Johnson said all of this began in 1919 when Einstein's discovery of relativity in the field of physical sciences was confused with the notion of relativism in the field of ideas. Johnson says that gradually, through the 1920s and 1930s, people began to challenge what had been the fixed assumptions by which people lived—the set of fixed and shared common values.

In the 1960s it exploded. Those of you who were on college campuses in the sixties will well remember that the writings of Camus and Sartre invaded American campuses. Basically, they were what Camus said when he came to America and spoke at Columbia University

SELF-OBSESSION

DESTROYS

CHARACTER.

in 1947. To the student body assembled he said, "There is nothing." The idea was introduced that there is no God. In this view there is no transcendent value; life is utterly meaningless, and the only way that we can derive meaning out of life is if we overcome the nothingness of life with heroic individualism. The goal of life is to overcome that nothingness and to find personal peace and meaning through your own autonomous efforts.

Most of the people of my generation dismissed what was happening on the campuses as a passing fad—a protest. It was *not*. The only people who behaved logically in the sixties were the flower children. They did exactly what they were taught; if there were no other object in life than to overcome the nothingness, then go out and smoke pot, make love, and enjoy personal peace.

Then, America came through the great convulsion of Watergate and Vietnam—a dark

CHARLES COLSON
The Line Between
Right
Wrong

17

era—and into the seventies. We thought we shook off those protest movements of the sixties. We did not; we simply embraced them into the mainstream of American culture. That's what gave rise to the "me" decade.

If you look at the bestsellers of the 1970s, they are very revealing: *Winning Through Intimidation, Looking Out for Number One*, and *I'm Okay, You're Okay*. Each of these were saying, "Don't worry about *us*." We emerged into a decade that Tom Wolfe, the social critic, called "the decade of Me." Very logically that graduated into the 1980s and what some have cynically called "the golden age of greed."

Sociologist Robert Bellah wrote a book titled *Habits of the Heart*—a phrase he borrowed from Tocqueville's classic work on American life. Bellah examined the values of several hundred average, middle-class Americans. He came to the conclusion that the

THE CRISIS OF CHARACTER IS TOTALLY UNDERSTANDABLE WHEN THERE ARE NO ABSOLUTE VALUES.

reigning ethos in American life in the eighties was what he called "ontological individualism," a radical individualism where the individual is supreme and autonomous and lives for himself or herself. He found that Americans had two overriding goals: vivid personal feelings and personal success.

Bellah tried to find out what people expected from the institutions of society. From business they expected personal advancement. Okay, that's fair enough. From marriage, personal development. No wonder marriages are in trouble. And from church, personal fulfillment! But the "personal" became the dominant consideration.

Now, I would simply say—and I'll try to be as brief with this as I possibly can—that this self-obsession destroys character. It has to! All of those quaint-sounding virtues I talked about, which historically have been considered the elements of character, are no match for a society in which the exaltation and gratification of self becomes the overriding goal of life.

Rolling Stone magazine surveyed members of the baby-boom generation, to which many of you emerging leaders in this room belong. Forty percent said there was no cause for which they would fight for their country. If there's nothing worth dying for, there's nothing worth living for. Literally the social contract unravels when that happens, and there can be no ethics.

How can you have ethical behavior? The crisis of character is totally understandable when there are no absolute values. The word *ethics* derives from the Greek word *ethos,* which literally meant "stall"—a hiding place. It was the one place you could go and find security. There could be rest and something that you could depend upon; it was immovable.

Morals derives from the word *mores,*

Ethics is not
—*CANNOT* be—
democratic.
Ethics by its very
definition is
authoritarian.

which means "always changing." *Ethics* or *ethos* is the normative; what *ought* to be. "Morals" is what *is*. Unfortunately, in American life today we are totally guided by moral determinations.

CHARLES COLSON
The Line Between
Right & Wrong

So, we're not even looking at ethical standards. Ethical standards don't change. It's the *stall,* it's the ethos, it's the environment in which we live. Morals change all the time. So, with shifting morals, if 90 percent of the people say that it's perfectly all right to do this, then that must be perfectly all right to do because 90 percent of the people say it is. It's a very democratic notion.

Ethics is not—*cannot* be—democratic. Ethics by its very definition is authoritarian. That's a very nasty word to utter on any campus in America, and particularly at Harvard, where Arthur Schlesinger has written a magnificently argued assault on the perils of absolutism.

CHARLES COLSON
The Line Between
Right & Wrong

In a relativistic environment ethics deteriorates to nothing more than utilitarian or pragmatic considerations. If you're really honest with yourselves and look at the ethical questions you're asked to wrestle with in your courses here at Harvard, you will see that you are being taught how to arrive at certain conclusions yourself, and to make certain judgments yourself, which ultimately are going to be good for business. That's fine, and you should do that. That's a prudential decision that has to be made. That's being a responsible business leader. It just isn't ethics and shouldn't be confused with ethics.

Ethics is what *ought* to be, not what is, or even what is prudential.

There was a brilliant professor at Duke University, Stanley Hauerwas, who wrote that "moral life cannot be found by each person pursuing his or her options." In relativism, all you have is a set of options. The only way

Ethics is
What *OUGHT* TO BE,
NOT WHAT IS,
OR EVEN WHAT IS
PRUDENTIAL.

moral life can be produced is by the formation by virtuous people of traditional communities. That was the accepted wisdom of Western civilization until the cultural revolution of the sixties, with which we are still plagued.

What is the answer? I'd like to address two points: first, how each of us, individually, might view our own ethical framework, and second, why some set of transcendent values is vital.

We live in a pluralistic society. I happen to be a Baptist—and believe *strongly* that, in a pluralistic environment, I should be able to contend for my values as you should be able to contend for your values, and out of that contention can come some consensus we can all agree to live by. That's the beauty of pluralism. It doesn't mean extinguishing all ideas; it means contending for them and finding truth out of that consensus.

Out of that battle comes some consensus

by which people live. But I would argue that there must be some values; and I would take the liberty of arguing for my belief in a certain set of historic values being absolutely essential to the survival of society.

First, let me address the question of how we find it ourselves. If you studied philosophy courses as an undergraduate, you read about Immanuel Kant and the categorical imperative. You read about rationalism and the ways in which people can find their own ethical framework. I guess the only thing I can tell you is that in my life—and I can't speak for anyone else—it didn't work.

I grew up in America during the Great Depression and thought that the great goal of life was success, material gain, power, and influence. That's why I went into politics. I believed I could gain power and influence how people lived. If I earned a law degree— as I did at night—and accumulated academic

CHARLES COLSON
The Line Between
Right & Wrong

honors and awards, it would enable me to find success, power, fulfillment, and meaning in life.

I had a great respect for the law. When I went through law school, I had a love for the law. I learned the history of jurisprudence and the philosophy underlying it.

I studied Locke, the Enlightenment, and social contract theories as an undergraduate at Brown, and had a great respect for the political process. I also had a well-above-average I.Q. and some academic honors. I became very self-righteous.

When I went to the White House, I gave up a law practice that was making almost $200,000 a year (and that was back in 1969, which wasn't bad in those days). It's kind of ordinary now for graduates of Harvard Business School, but then it was a lot of money.

I had accumulated a little bit of money, so I took a job in the White House at $40,000 a year. I took everything I had and I stuck it in a blind trust at the Bank of Boston. Now let me tell you, if you want to lose money, that's the surest way to do it! After three and a half years, when I saw what the Bank of Boston had done to my blind trust, I realized I was a lot poorer when I came out of the government than I was when I went *into* the government.

But there was one thing about which I was absolutely certain—that no one could corrupt me. *Positive!* And if anybody ever gave me a present at Christmas time, it went right to the driver of my limousine. They used to send in bottles of whiskey, boxes of candy, and all sorts of things. Right to the driver of my automobile. I wouldn't accept a thing.

Patty and I were taken out on someone's boat one day. I discovered it was a chartered boat, and ended up paying for half of it because I didn't want to give the appearance of impropriety. Imagine me, worried about things

CHARLES COLSON
The Line Between
Right & Wrong

CHARLES COLSON
The Line Between
Right & Wrong

like that!

I ended up going to prison. So much for the categorical imperative. The categorical imperative says that with our own rational process we will arrive at that judgment which, if everyone did it, would be prudential and the best decision for everyone. In other words, that which we would do, we would do only if we could will it to be a universal choice for everybody.

I really thought that way, and I never once in my life thought I was breaking the law. I would have been *terrified* to do it because I would jeopardize the law degree I had worked four years at night to earn. I had worked my way onto the Law Review, Order of Coif, and Moot Court—all the things that lawyers do— and I graduated in the top of my class. I wouldn't put that in jeopardy for anything in the world!

EVERY HUMAN BEING HAS
AN INFINITE CAPACITY FOR
SELF-RATIONALIZATION
AND
SELF-DELUSION.

CHARLES COLSON
The Line Between
Right & Wrong

I was so sure. But, you see, there are two problems. Every human being has an infinite capacity for self-rationalization and self-delusion. You get caught up in a situation where you are absolutely convinced that the fate of the republic *rests* on the reelection of, in my case, Richard Nixon. I'm sure that next year people will think the same thing about George Bush. There's an *enormous* amount of peer pressure, and you don't take time to stop and think, *Wait a minute. Is this* right *by some absolute standard or does this seem right in the circumstances? Is it okay?*

I was taught to think clearly and carefully. As a lawyer that's what you do—you briefcase it, you spend four years in law school, and you go like a monkey. You're briefing cases, briefing cases. We used the case method, as you use the case method here in business. The case method in law school, however, is a little bit different, because you always have a fixed conclusion, so at least I knew there was a fixed law that you would arrive at. I had all the mental capacity to do that. I was capable of infinite self-delusion.

Second, and even more important—and this goes to the heart of the ethical dilemma in America today—even if I had known I was doing wrong, would I have had the *will* to do what is right? It isn't hindsight. I have to tell you the answer to that is no.

The greatest myth of the twentieth century is that people are good. We aren't. We're not morally neutral. My great friend, Professor Stan Samenow, happens to be an orthodox Jew. I asked him one day, "Stan, if people were put in a room and no one could see what they were doing or no one knew what they were doing, would they do the right thing half the time and the wrong thing half the time? Would they do the wrong thing all the time, or would they do the right thing all the time?" He

CHARLES COLSON
The Line Between
Right
Wrong

THE GREATEST MYTH
OF THE TWENTIETH CENTURY IS
THAT PEOPLE ARE GOOD.

said they would *always* do the wrong thing.

We aren't morally neutral. I know that's a terribly unpopular thing to say in America today, but it happens to be true. The fundamental problem with learning how to reason through ethical solutions is that it doesn't give you a mechanism to override your natural tendency to do what is wrong. This is what C.S. Lewis—whose writings have had such a profound influence on my life—says.

My blessed friend Tom Phillips gave me the book *Mere Christianity* when I came to him in the summer of 1973 at a moment of great anguish in my life. I wasn't so worried about what was going on in Watergate, but I knew I didn't like what was going on in my heart. But something was different about him. So I went to see him one evening.

I went, and that was the evening that this ex-Marine captain, White House tough guy, Nixon hatchet man (and all kinds of things

CHARLES COLSON
The Line Between
Right Wrong

CHARLES COLSON
The Line Between
Right & Wrong

you can't write about in print or wouldn't say in polite company that I was called in those days—much of it justifiably) found myself unable to drive the automobile out of the driveway when I left his home, after he had told me of his experience with Jesus Christ. I was crying too hard.

I took that little book he had given me, *Mere Christianity*, and began to read it and study it as I would study for a case. I'd take my yellow legal pad and get down all the arguments—both sides. I was confronted with the most powerful mind that I had ever been exposed to, I saw the arguments for the truth of Jesus Christ, and I surrendered my life eighteen years ago. My life has not been the same since and can never be the same again.

I discovered that Christ coming into your life changes that will. It gives you that will to do what you know is right, where even if you know what is right—and most of the time

WE MOCK HONOR —
AND THEN WE ARE ALARMED
WHEN THERE ARE
TRAITORS IN OUR MIDST.

you won't—you don't have the *will* to do it. It's what C.S. Lewis wrote in that tremendous little book, *Abolition of Man*. I'd love you to read *Mere Christianity*, but if you had to read just *Mere Christianity* or *Abolition of Man* for today's cultural environment, read *Abolition of Man*. Wonderful book.

I don't know how to say this in language that is inclusive, but he wrote a marvelous essay called "Men Without Chests." It's a wonderful article about the will. He said the intellect can't control the passions of the stomach except by means of the will—which is the chest. But we mock honor—and then we are alarmed when there are traitors in our midst. It is like making geldings, he said, and then bidding them to multiply. He was talking about the loss of character in 1947 and 1948, long before the results we are witnessing today of the loss of character in American life.

So much for the individual. What about

society as a whole? Margaret Thatcher delivered what I consider to be one of the most remarkable speeches in modern times two and a half years ago before the Church of Scotland. You'll find it reprinted only in the *Wall Street Journal.* Margaret Thatcher said—and I'll paraphrase that marvelous, eloquent speech —that the truth of the Judeo-Christian tradition is infinitely precious, not only because she believes it to be true—and she professed her own faith—but also, she said, because it provides the moral impulse that causes people to rise above themselves and do something greater than themselves, without which a democracy cannot survive. She went on to make the case—I think quite convincingly—that without Judeo-Christian values at the root of society, society simply can't exist.

Our founders believed this. We were not formed as a totally tolerant, neutral, egalitarian democracy. We were formed as a republic with

CHARLES COLSON
The Line Between
Right
Wrong

WE DO
GOOD THINGS BECAUSE
THERE IS
SOMETHING IN US THAT
CALLS US TO
SOMETHING GREATER
THAN OURSELVES.

a certain sense of republican virtue built into the citizenry, without which limited government simply couldn't survive. No one said it better than John Adams: "Our constitution was made only for a moral and religious people. It is wholly inadequate for the government of any other."

CHARLES COLSON
The Line Between
Right &Wrong

There are four ways in which that moral impulse works. Someone sent me a letter suggesting the topic for this speech, "Why Good People Do Bad Things." I didn't have time to write back and say I really think that it would be more appropriate to address "Why Bad People Do Good Things," because that's a more difficult question.

Why do we do good things? If we live in an age of ontological individualism, if radical individualism is the pervasive ethos of the day, if we simply live for the gratification of our senses, of our personal success, and vivid personal feelings, why do anything good?

CHARLES COLSON
The Line Between
Right Wrong

Who cares? It won't make a particle of difference unless it's important to your balance sheet. But that's pragmatism, that isn't doing good things. That's pure utilitarianism.

First, we do good things because there is something in us that calls us to something greater than ourselves.

Prison Fellowship is, of course, a ministry in the prisons—not a very glamorous place to be. I visited three prisons this weekend. I was so moved in one prison because there were six hundred inmates that came out and saw their lives change. Now those were people who were lost and forgotten. One man stood up and said, "Ten years ago I was in this prison, and two of your volunteers came in, Mr. Colson, and they befriended me, this couple from Akron, Ohio." He said, "You know, they've been visiting me every month and writing to me ever since, for ten years." He continued, "I get out of prison in September, and they've invited me to live in their home." He said, "I'm going to make it."

Why do people do things like this? Why do they go to the AIDS wards? One of my friends goes into the AIDS ward of a prison all of the time, and people die in his arms. Do we do it because we have some good instinct? No! It's a moral impulse.

Why did William Wilberforce stand up on the floor of the Parliament in the House of Commons and denounce the slave trade? He said it was barbaric and cost himself the prime ministership of England when he said it! But, he said, I have no choice as a Christian. He spent the next twenty years battling the slave trade and brought it to an end in England because of his Christian conscience.

What is it that makes us, as otherwise self-centered people disposed to evil—if the history of the twentieth century and civilization is correct—what is it that makes us do good?

CHARLES COLSON
The Line Between
Right & Wrong

CHARLES COLSON
The Line Between
Right
&Wrong

Second, Margaret Thatcher is absolutely right. A society cannot survive without a moral consensus.

I tell you this as one who sat next to the president of the United States and observed our nation's fragile moral consensus during the Vietnam era. We did some excessive things, and we were wrong. But we did it feeling that if we didn't, the whole country was going to fall apart. It was like a banana republic having the 82nd Airborne down in the basement of the White House. One night my car was fire-bombed on the way home. They had 250,000 protesters in the streets: You almost wondered if the White House was going to be overrun.

The moral consensus that holds our country together was in great peril during that era and during the entire Watergate aftermath of Vietnam. A free society can't exist without it.

Now, what gives it to us? Thomas Aquinas wrote that without moral consensus, there

THE REASON WE HAVE
THE MOST TERRIBLE CRIME
PROBLEM IN THE WORLD
IN AMERICA TODAY
IS SIMPLE:
WE'VE LOST OUR
MORAL CONSENSUS.
WE'RE PEOPLE LIVING
FOR OURSELVES.

CHARLES COLSON
The Line Between
Right & Wrong

can be no law. Chairman Mao gave the other side of that in saying that morality begins at the muzzle of a gun. Every society has two choices: whether it wants to be ruled by an authoritarian ruler, or whether there can be a set of shared values and certain things we hold in common that give us the philosophical underpinnings of our value system in our life.

I submit to you that without that—call it natural law if you wish, call it Judeo-Christian revelation, call it the accumulated wisdom of twenty-three centuries of Western civilization—I don't believe a society can exist.

The reason we have the most terrible crime problem in the world in America today is simple: We've lost our moral consensus. We're people living for ourselves.

We doubled the prison population in America during the 1980s. We are today number one in the rate of incarceration per capita in the world. When I started Prison Fellowship fifteen years ago, the U.S. was number three. We trailed the Soviet Union and South Africa. Today we're number one. While we build more prisons and put more people in, the recidivism rate remains constant at 74 percent. Those people go right back in.

CHARLES COLSON
The Line Between

The answer to it is very simple. There are kids being raised today from broken families who are not being given values. Remember that Stanley Hauerwas said the way you foster ethics is in tradition-formed communities. They're not being given values in the home, they're not being given values in the school, they're watching the television set for seven hours and thirty-six minutes a day, and what they're seeing is, "you only go around once, so grab for all the gusto you can." Now if that's the creed by which you live, then at twelve years old you're out on the streets sniffing coke. We arrest them and put them in jail.

CHARLES COLSON

The Line Between

Right & Wrong

They think we're crazy. So do I.

Until you have some desire in society to live by a different set of values, we'll be building prisons in America until, as is the case today, 25 percent of the black, male inner-city population in America is either in prison or on probation or parole. We can't make it without that moral consensus. It will cost us dearly if we can't find a way to restore it.

Professor James Wilson, formerly at Harvard Law School, wrote one of the most telling pieces I've ever read, and I refer to it in one of my books, *Kingdoms in Conflict*. He wrote a primer, while he was here at Harvard, about the relationship between spiritual values and crime. It is really interesting.

The prevailing myth is that crime goes up during periods of poverty. Actually, it went down during the 1930s. He found that, during periods of industrialization, it went up as what he called Victorian values began to fade. When

EVEN THE MOST
RATIONAL APPROACH
TO ETHICS IS
DEFENSELESS
IF THERE ISN'T
THE WILL TO DO
WHAT IS RIGHT.

CHARLES COLSON

The Line Between

Right & Wrong

there was a resurgence of spiritual values, crime went down. He saw a direct correlation. Crime went up whenever spiritual values went down; when spiritual values went up, crime went down.

Third, I think we often miss the basis of sound policy because we have become secularized in our views in America and afraid to look at biblical revelation. We're terrified of it.

When Ted Koppel gave the commencement speech at Duke University a few years ago, in which he said the Ten Commandments weren't the Ten Suggestions, and that God handed the Commandments to Moses at Mt. Sinai, you know what the press did to him. It was horrible. A fellow like Ted Koppel couldn't possibly say something like that! So we blind ourselves to what can often be truth.

I have spoken to over half of the state legislators in America and have spoken with many of the political leaders around this country. I always make the same argument to them about our prisons. We have way too many people in prison. Half of them are in for non-violent offenses, which to me is ludicrous. They should be put to work. People should not be sitting in a cell at a cost of $20,000 a year to taxpayers while doing absolutely nothing, and while their victims get no recompense. Offenders ought to be put in a work program paying back their victims. Whenever I speak about that, the response I get from political officials is amazing. It really is.

In the Texas legislature, I gave that talk and they all applauded. Afterward the Speaker of the House said, "Mr. Colson, wait here. I'm sure some of the members would like to talk to you." They came flooding in afterward. They all said that restitution is a wonderful idea—where did that come from? I asked, "Have you got a Bible at home?" They say, "Have I got a Bible at home?" "Well," I responded, "you go

home and dust it off and you'll see that's exactly what God told Moses on Mt. Sinai."

That's biblical truth. That's the lesson of Jesus and Zacchaeus. We blind ourselves to it because we think there's something wrong with that in today's tolerant society. But in a pluralistic society that ought not to be wrong. We ought to be seeking that out. If we can find wisdom, find it. So often we find wisdom in the teachings of the Holy Scripture.

Fourth, no society exists in a vacuum. Vacuums don't remain vacuums—they get filled. In a vacuum, a tyrant will often emerge. You've just seen seventy years of that crumble in the former Soviet Union. Isn't it interesting that when it crumbles, it so often crumbles because people have an allegiance to a power above the power of that earthly potentate?

I remember when Pope John Paul II said that he would return to Poland if the Soviets invaded during Poland's period of martial law in the early eighties. Years earlier Stalin had said, "Hah! The Pope! How many divisions does he have?" Well, as a result of the Solidarity movement, we saw how many divisions he had—a whole lot more than the Soviets.

I remember getting on a plane and coming up to Boston to see our first grandson when he was born, back in 1981. A man got up in the aisle of the plane and was all excited to see me. He said, "Chuck Colson!" He was blocking the people coming behind me, so I finally got him into his seat.

He was talking so fast that I couldn't understand him. To make a long story short, he introduced himself as Benigno Aquino.

Aquino told me that when he was in jail for seven years and seven months, as a political prisoner of Marcos, he had read my book *Born Again*. He was in a prison cell and had gotten down on his knees and surrendered

CHARLES COLSON
The Line Between
Right & Wrong

his life to Jesus Christ. He said after that his entire experience in prison changed. Well, Nino and I became pretty good friends. We did some television programs together, and we visited frequently.

He called me up one day and said, "I'm going back to the Philippines." I said, "Nino, do you think that's wise?" He said, "I have to. I'm going back because my conscience will not let me do otherwise." He was safe here in America, he had a fellowship at Harvard, he could lecture anywhere he wanted. He and his wife had everything they could possibly want.

But he knew he had to go back to the Philippines. "My conscience will not let me do otherwise." He said, "If I go to jail, it'll be okay, I'll be president of Prison Fellowship in the Philippines." He said, "If there are free elections, I'll be elected president. I know I can beat Marcos. And if I'm killed, I know I'll be with Jesus Christ." He went back in total freedom.

And he was shot and killed as he got off the airplane.

But an extraordinary thing happened—what's known as people power. People went out into the streets. The tanks stopped. People went up and put flowers down the muzzles of guns: A tyrant was overthrown. A free government was reasserted because people believed in a power above themselves.

I was in the former Soviet Union last year and visited five prisons, four of which had never been visited by anyone from the West. I met with Soviet officials. It was really interesting. I met with Vadim Bakatin, then minister of interior affairs. When talking about the enormous crime problem in the Soviet Union, he said to me, "What are we going to do about it?" I said, "Mr. Bakatin, your problem is exactly the one that Fyodor Dostoyevsky, your great novelist, diagnosed. In *Brothers Karamazov,* he had that debate between the older brother,

H OW FOOLISH WE ARE

IN AMERICA

TO BE SQUANDERING

OUR HERITAGE.

who is unregenerate, and the younger brother, Alexis, who is the priest, over the soul of the middle brother, Ivan. At one point, Ivan yells out and says, "*Ah, if there is no God, everything is permissible.*" Crime becomes inevitable. I said, "Your problem in the Soviet Union is seventy years of atheism." He said, "You're right. We need what you're talking about. How do we get it back in the Soviet Union?"

All I could think was how foolish we are in America to be squandering our heritage. In a country where they've ignored the king of greater power for seventy years, they're losing it all.

I can only leave you with a very simple message, as someone who had thought he had it all together and attained a position of great power. I never thought I'd be one of the half-dozen men sitting around the desk of the president of the United States, with all of that power and influence. I discovered that there

CHARLES COLSON
The Line Between
Right Wrong

was no restraint on the evil in me. In my self-righteousness, I was never more dangerous.

I discovered what Solzhenitsyn wrote so brilliantly from a prison—that the line between good and evil passes not between principalities and powers, but it oscillates within the human heart. Even the most rational approach to ethics is defenseless if there isn't the will to do what is right. On my own—and I can only speak for myself—I do not have that will. That which I want to do, I do not do; that which I do, I do not want to do.

It's only when I can turn to the One whom we celebrate at Easter—the One who was raised from the dead—that I can find the will to do what is right. It's only when that value and that sense of righteousness pervade a society that there can be a moral consensus. I would hope I might leave with you, as future business leaders, the thought that a society of which we are a part—and for which you

IT'S ONLY WHEN

I CAN TURN TO

THE ONE WHOM

WE CELEBRATE AT EASTER—

THE ONE WHO WAS

RAISED FROM THE DEAD—

THAT I CAN FIND THE WILL

TO DO WHAT IS RIGHT.

CHARLES COLSON
The Line Between
Right & Wrong

should have a great sense of responsibility and stewardship—desperately needs those kind of values. And, if I might say so, each one of us does as well.

About Prison Fellowship

Prison Fellowship is an interdenominational ministry to prisoners, ex-prisoners, and their families, founded in 1976 by Charles W. Colson. After serving seven months in prison for a Watergate-related offense, Colson devoted his life to working with prisoners and their families.

In 1976 he started Prison Fellowship with two staff members and three volunteers. Since that time, Prison Fellowship has grown phenomenally. Some 300 employees and almost 50,000 volunteers work in states across America. Prison Fellowship International has involvement with prison ministry groups in over seventy countries around the world.

Prison Fellowship believes that the first and most important step in true rehabilitation is a spiritual one—when an inmate consciously turns away from the old life to a new life in Jesus Christ. But that turning point is only the beginning. Inmates need teaching, guidance, and encouragement, as well as practical life skills. They need role models to help them see how to become respectable citizens who contribute to society. Prison Fellowship has a variety of in-prison and external programs to help accomplish these goals.

If you would like to support our cause or would like to learn more about Prison Fellowship, contact us at the following address:

Prison Fellowship Ministries
P.O. Box 97103
Washington, D.C. 20090-7103
703-478-0100
web site: http://www.pfm.org

Charles Colson is chairman of the board of Prison Fellowship, a ministry that exhorts and equips the church to help those suffering at all points in the cycle of crime. The author of such international bestsellers as *Born Again, Life Sentence, Kingdoms in Conflict,* and *The Body,* Mr. Colson is also a familiar voice with his Christian commentary, "BreakPoint."